Travel in the U.S.A.
THEN & NOW

Maya Franklin

Table of Contents

On the Go	3
By Land *Then*	4
By Land *Now*	7
By Sea *Then*	10
By Sea *Now*	13
By Sky *Then*	16
By Sky *Now*	18
What's Next?	20
Travel Inventions Time Line	22
Glossary	24

On the Go

Where would you like to go? How will you get there?

You have many choices. You can hop on a train, drive along a highway, fly in an airplane, or sail across the seas. You can even go by foot. There are so many ways to travel!

But did people always have so many choices?

Long ago, when the United States was a new country, travel was very different from what it is today. There were no trains, no planes, and no highways connecting each city to the next.

So, how did people get where they wanted to go?

By Land
Then

The truth is that long ago people did not travel much. It was difficult and expensive to travel. People stayed near their homes.

Most people lived in small towns or cities. If they wanted to go somewhere, they would walk, ride a horse, or drive wagons or carriages pulled by horses.

People made or grew most of what they needed, so they did not have much reason to leave home. If their families lived far away, they would not see them often.

Whoa!
Horses weren't the only animals people used for travel. Donkeys, mules, and oxen were ridden or used to pull wagons and carriages.

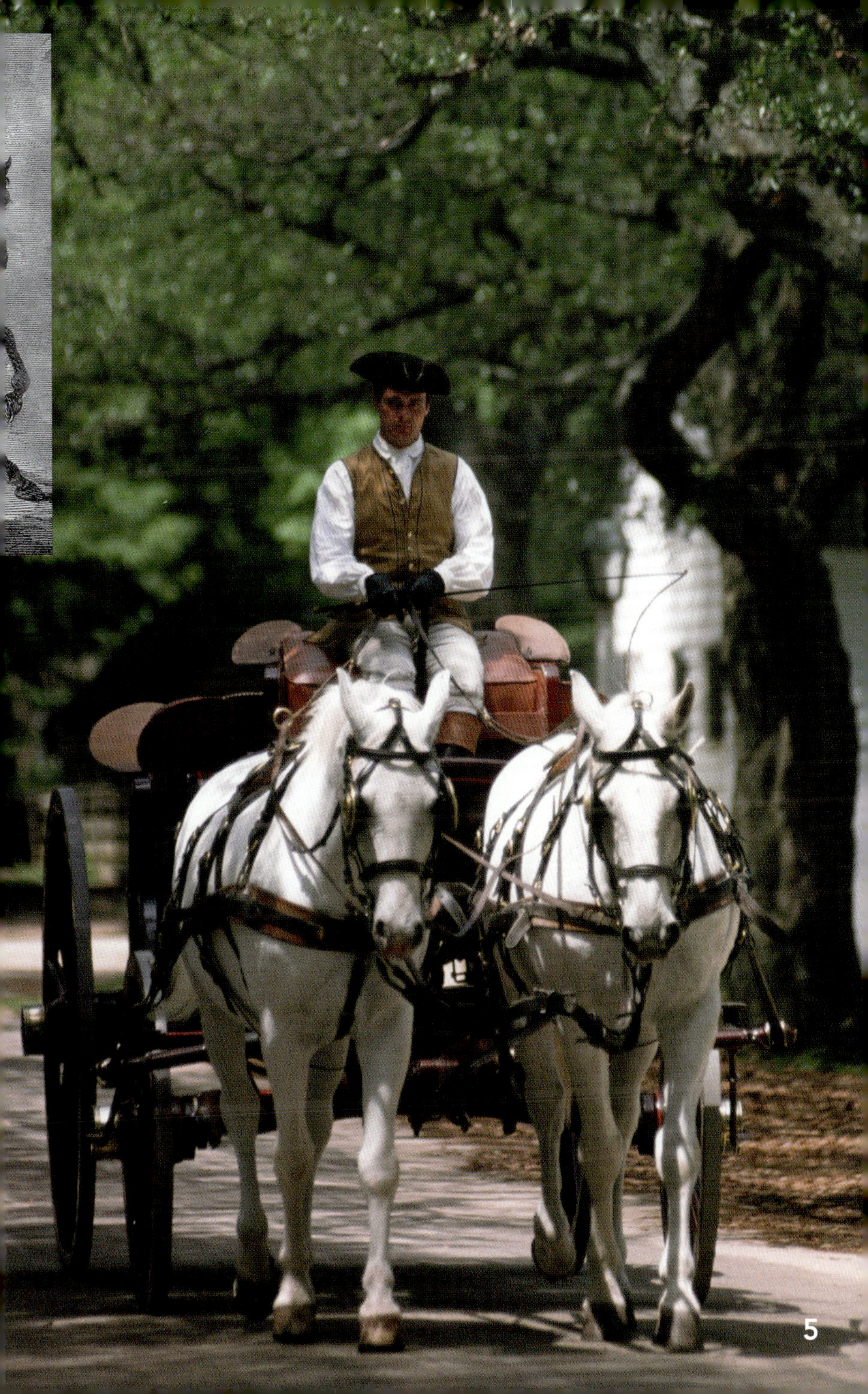

Most roads long ago were made of dirt. They were rocky, bumpy, and hard to travel. During wet weather, they became muddy and slippery.

In the winter, when snow and ice covered the roads, people sometimes rode in sleighs pulled by horses. Their sleighs did not have heaters like we have in cars today, so the travellers wrapped themselves in blankets.

Hot Potato!
You probably like to eat baked potatoes, but long ago, people sometimes used them to keep warm. While traveling in cold weather, they sometimes put hot potatoes in their coat pockets to warm their hands.

By Land
Now

Today, many people drive cars and trucks. They ride on paved roads that cross the country and are easy to use in rain or shine. Automobiles today have heaters and air conditioners. People travel miles and miles in just a short amount of time.

What Is an Automobile?
An **automobile** (ah-to-mo-BEEL) is a type of transportation for people. Automobiles have engines and can be driven on streets and highways.

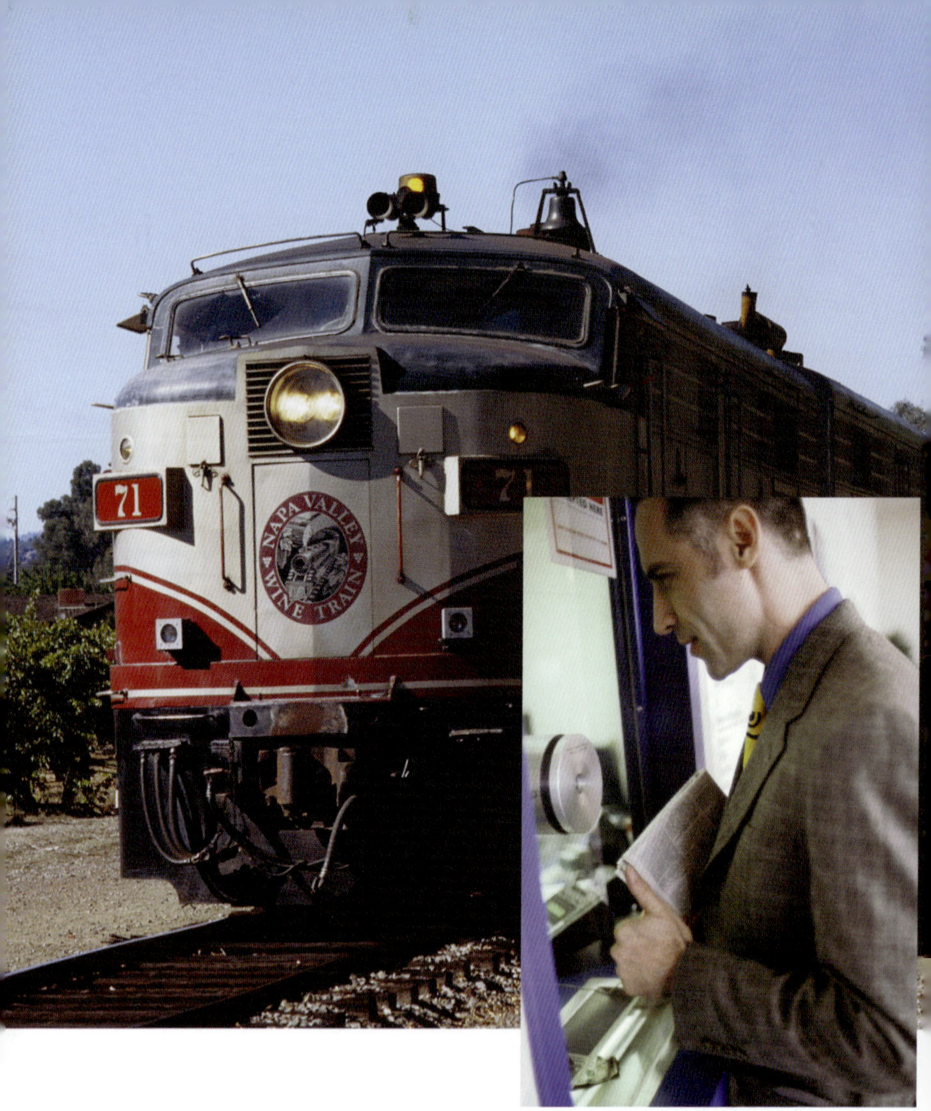
71
NAPA VALLEY
WINE TRAIN

People can also buy tickets to travel near and far. Many cities have buses and subways, and people can take trains almost anywhere in the country. They just buy a ticket and get on board!

Not many people keep horses today for travel. Years ago, horses were the power behind land travel. Now, horses are mainly kept for sport and fun. Gas and electricity are used for power when traveling.

5 Busiest Travel Days
Thanksgiving
54 million travelers
Christmas
47 million travelers
Fourth of July
46 million travelers
Easter
46 million travelers
Labor Day
45 million travelers
0
10
20
30
40
50
60
million travelers

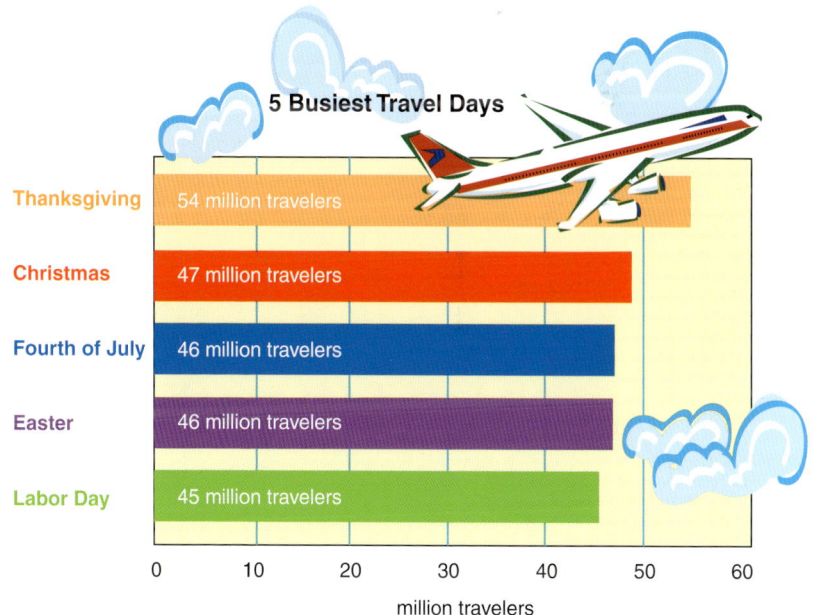

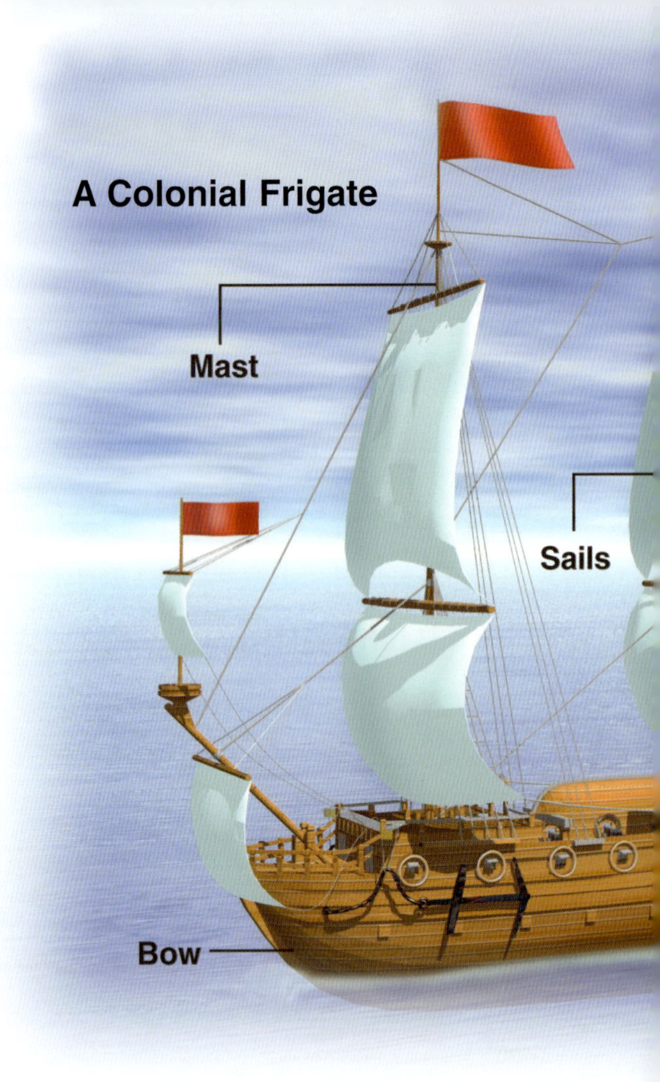
A Colonial Frigate
Mast
Sails
Bow

By Sea
Then

People have been traveling by boat for more than 60,000 years. But the types of boats have changed over time.

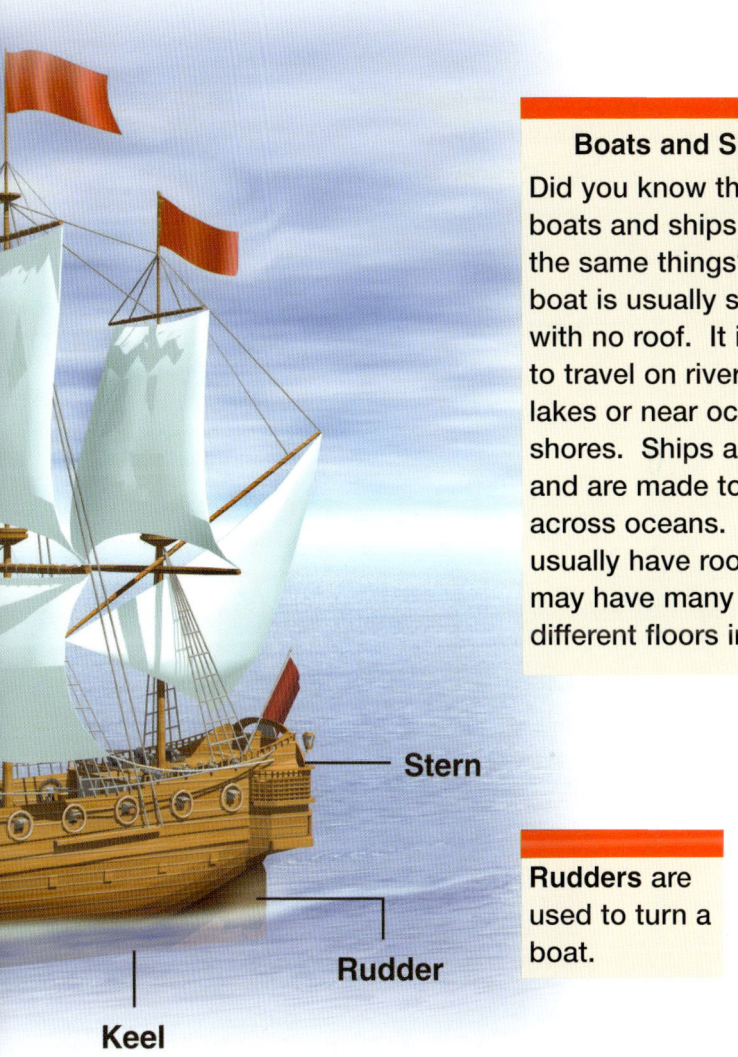

Stern

Rudder

Keel

Boats and Ships
Did you know that boats and ships are not the same things? A boat is usually small with no roof. It is used to travel on rivers and lakes or near ocean shores. Ships are large and are made to travel across oceans. They usually have roofs and may have many different floors inside.

Rudders are used to turn a boat.

In the early United States, boats had sails, oars, and **rudders** for steering and movement. There were no engines. Only wind and muscle power made boats go.

American Turtle

A **submarine** (sub-ma-REEN) is a boat that can travel underwater and come back up again. During the American Revolution, the American Turtle was sent underwater to attach a bomb to a British warship. The bomb did not work, but the submarine did!

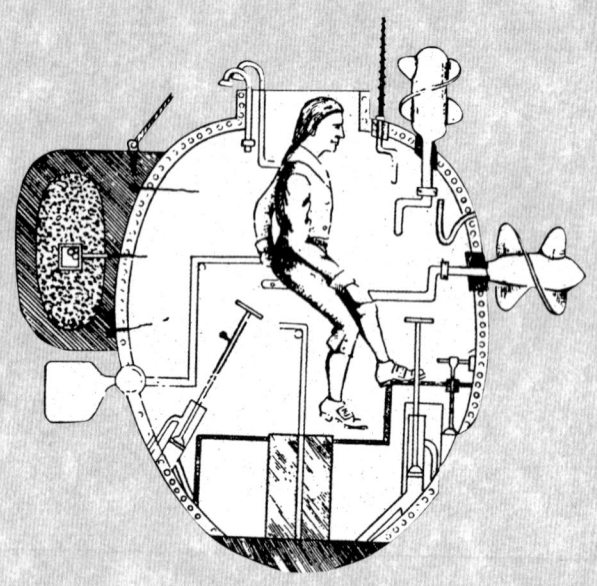

Lots of muscle power was needed for the first **submarine**! It was invented in 1776 and called the *American Turtle*. One person could fit inside. The person turned a crank to spin a propeller outside the submarine.

By Sea
Now

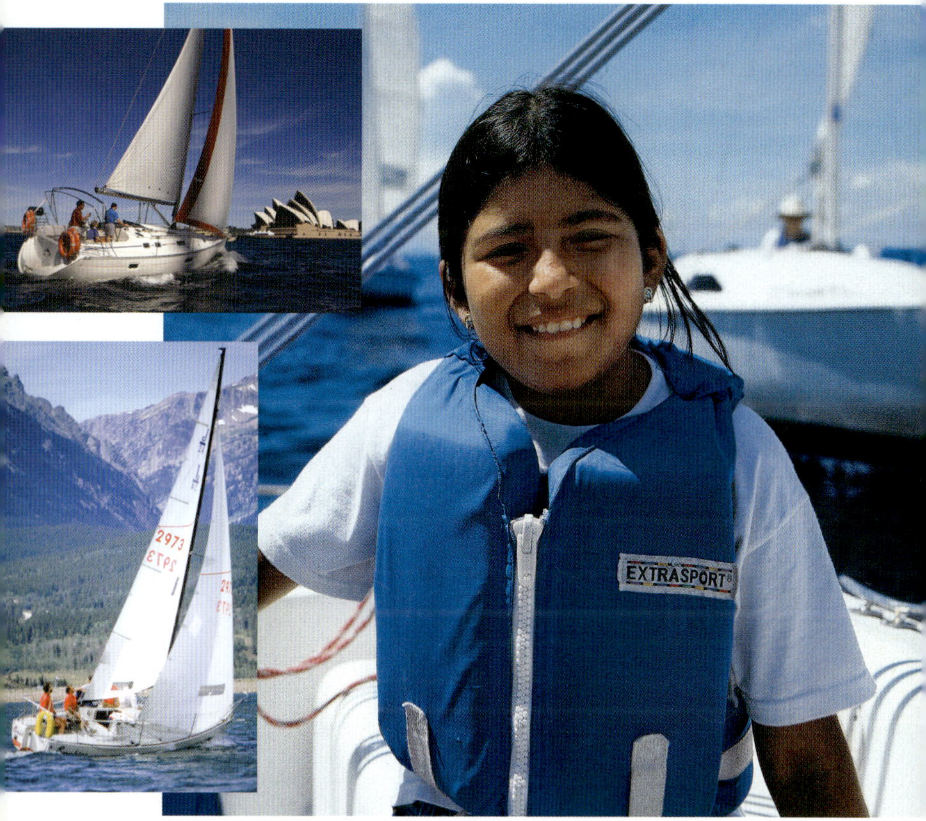
2973
EXTRASPORT

Boats and ships have many uses today. Some large ships carry supplies. Some carry people, and some boats are just for fun. People like to sail, fish, and race with their boats.

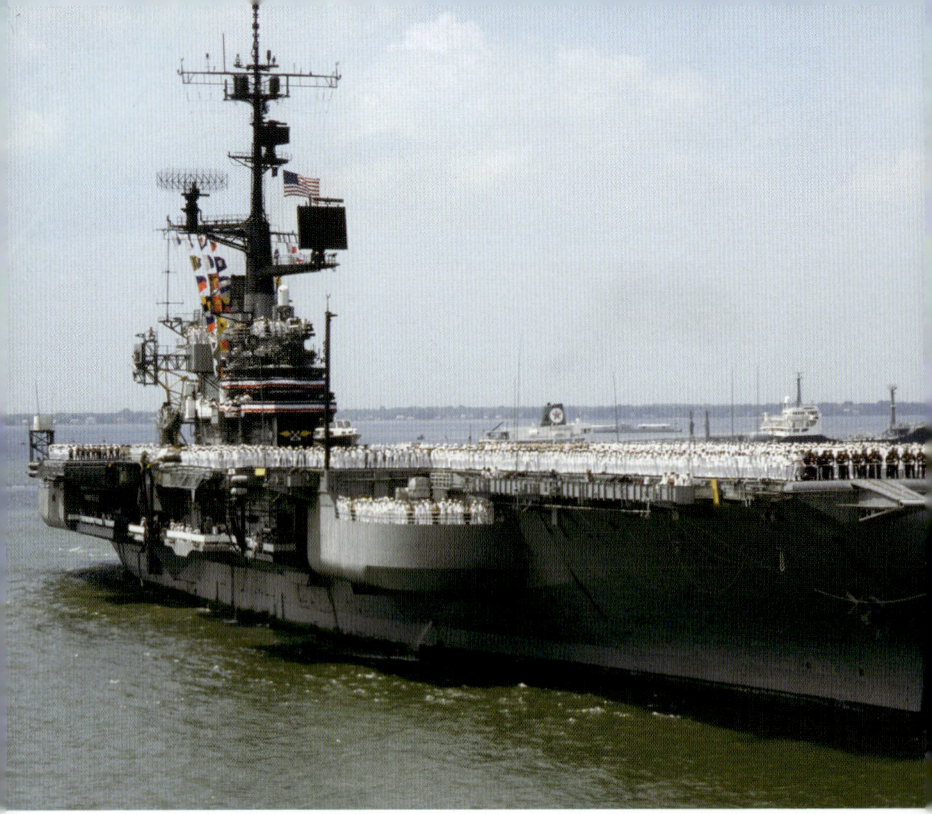

Boats today can go very fast, because now we have engines. But some people still use sails and oars.

Ships today are usually much bigger than ships long ago. Cruise ships can take hundreds of people across the oceans. Navies have large ships to bring soldiers all around the world.

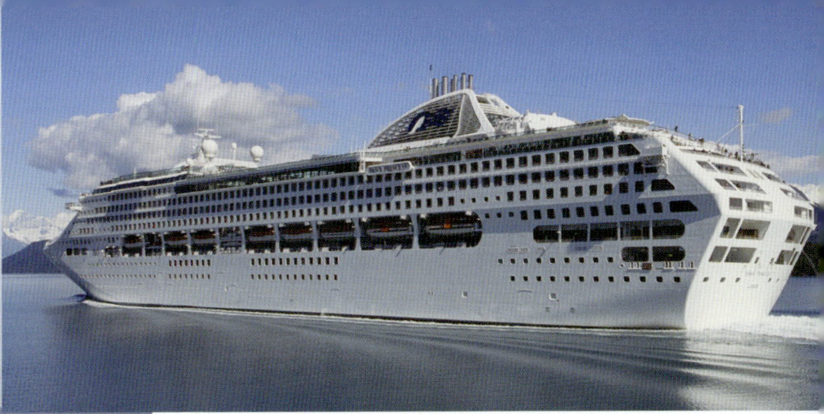

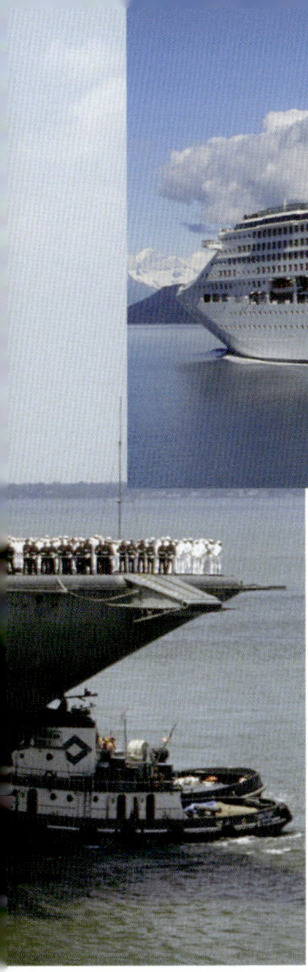

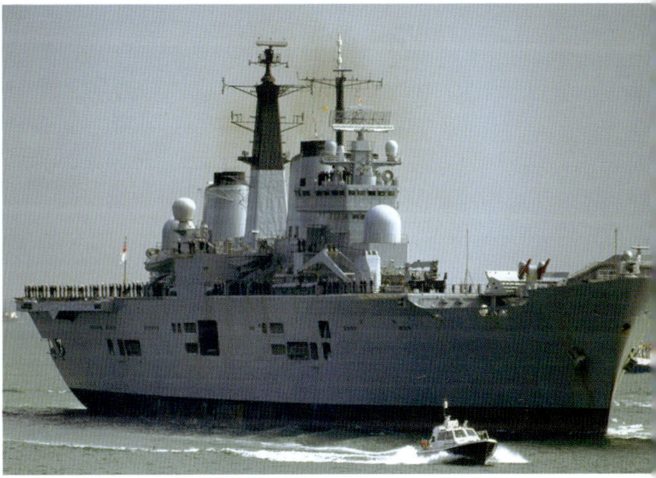

It is also easier for ships to find their way today. Now we have equipment so that sailors know exactly where they are and how to get where they are going. Long ago, the sun and the stars were all sailors had for directions.

By Sky
Then

Back when the United States was a young country, you might see birds flying in the sky but nothing else. Hot-air balloons and gliders would come soon, but airplanes were still many years away.

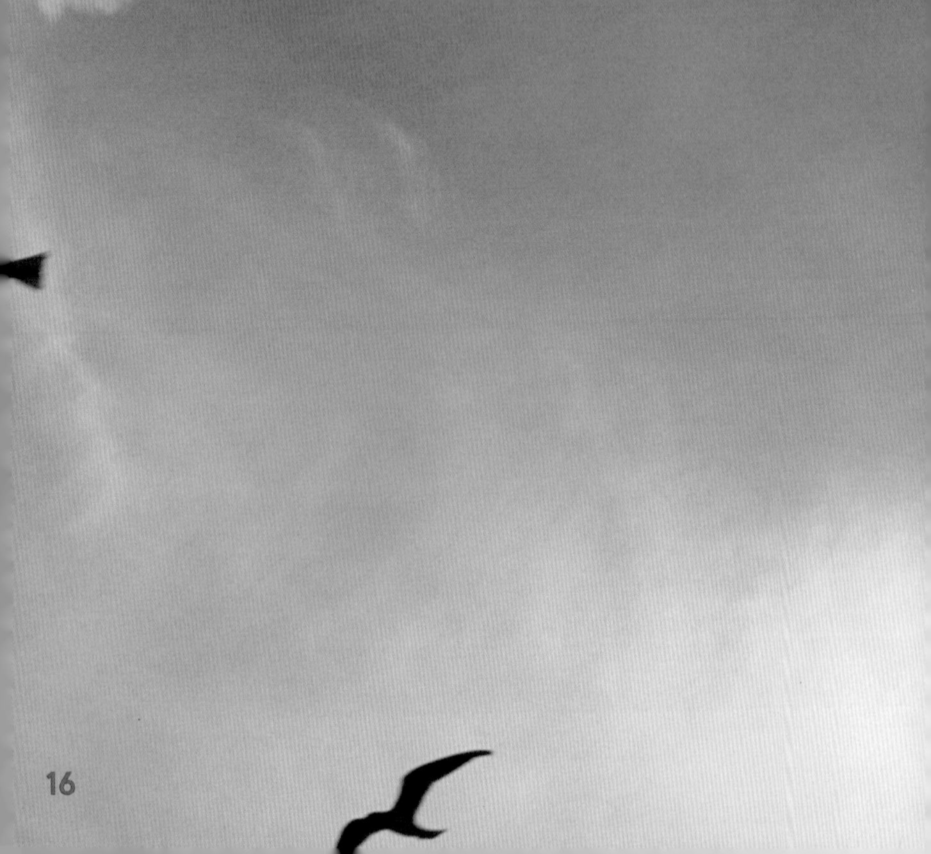

The Wright Brothers manned the first successful powered flight in 1903 at Kitty Hawk. The plane flew for 12 seconds.

By Sky *Now*

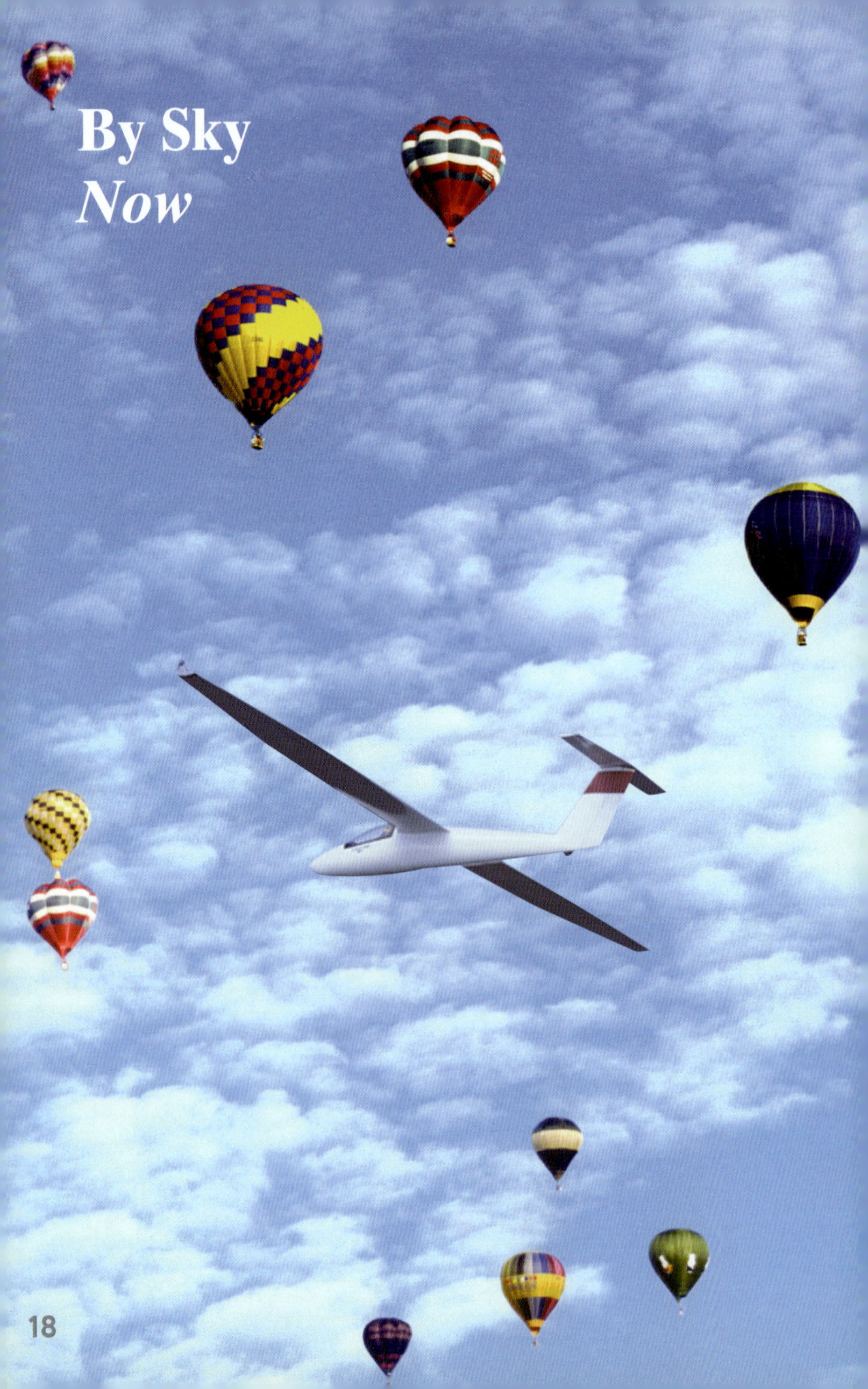

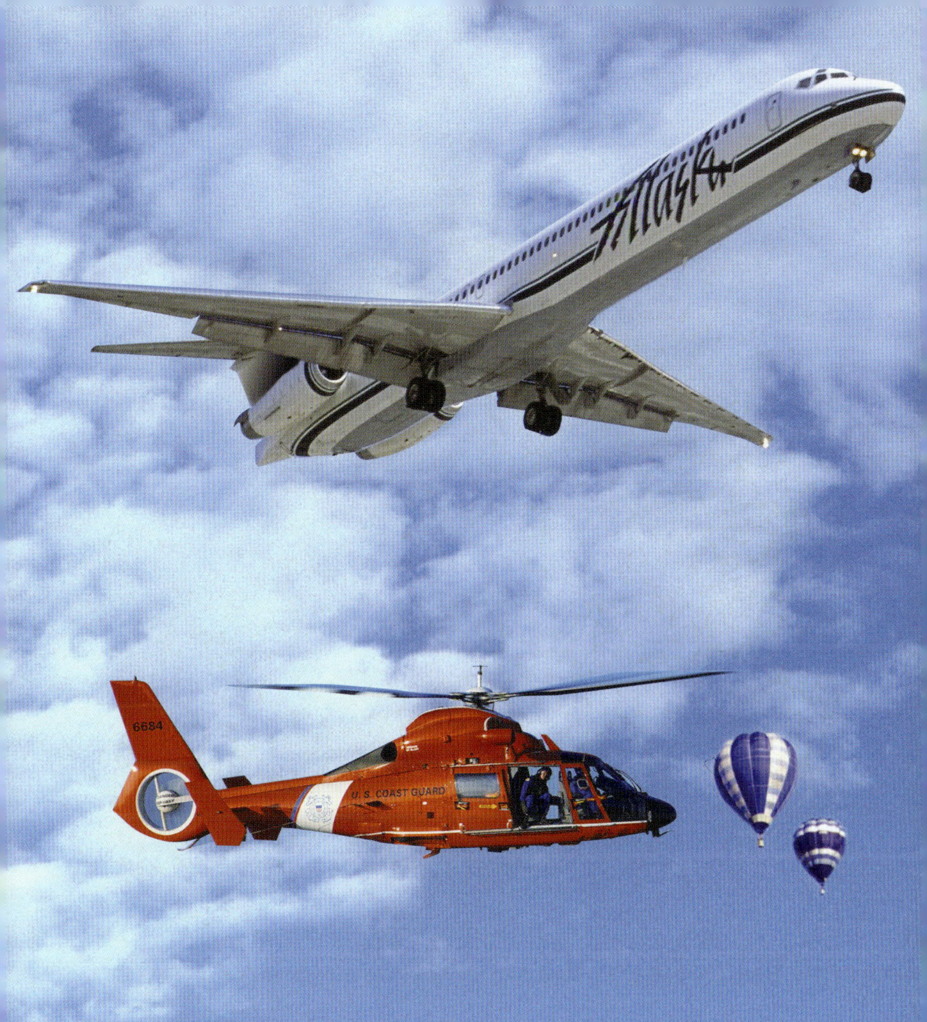
Alaska
6684
U.S. COAST GUARD

Now the sky is full of flying things. Airplanes fly from country to country. Helicopters whirl their propellers in the air. People fly in gliders and balloons just for fun. Spaceships soar to the moon and beyond.

What's Next?

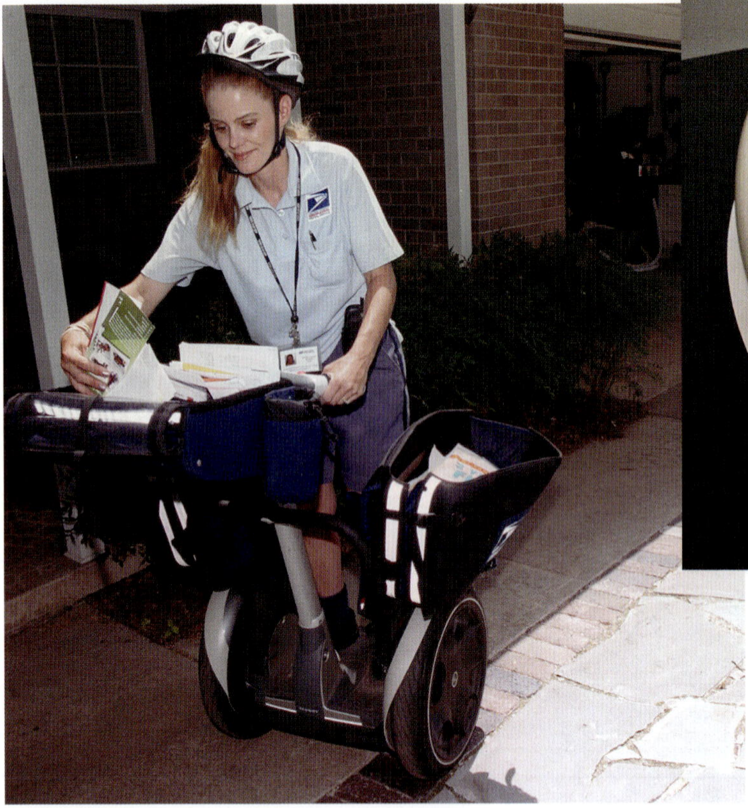

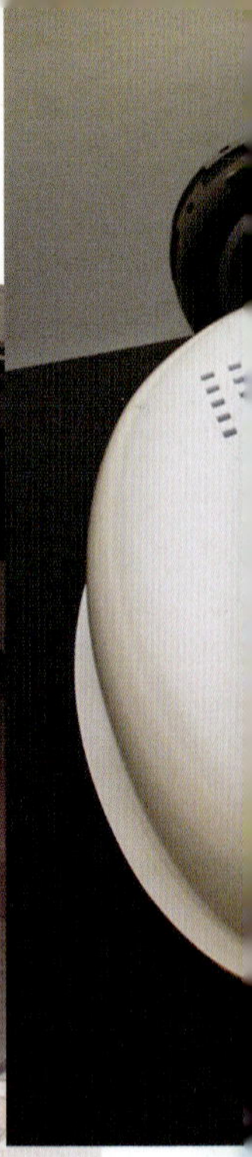

Travel has changed a lot over time, and there will be more changes in the future. It seems that if people can dream it, in time they can build it, too. By land, sea, or sky, anything is possible!

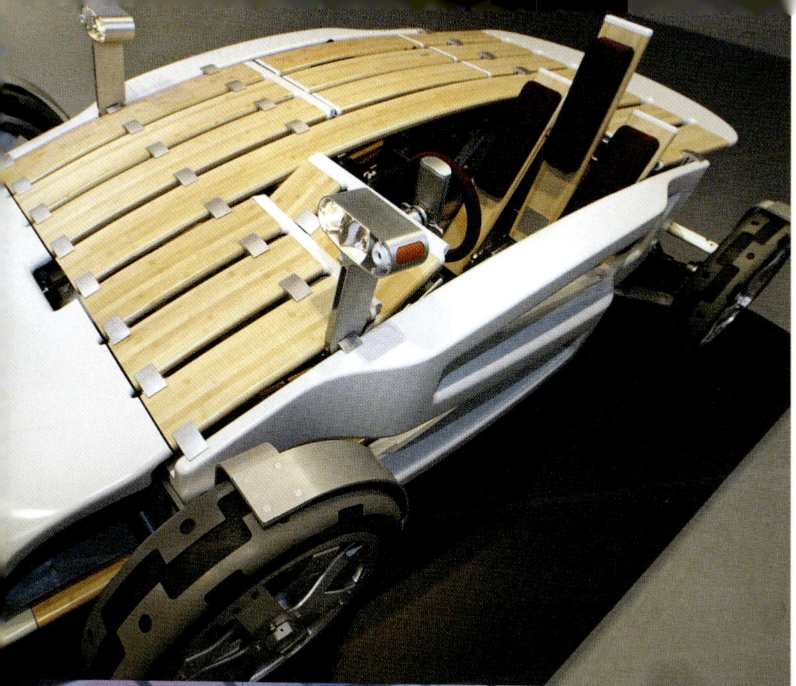

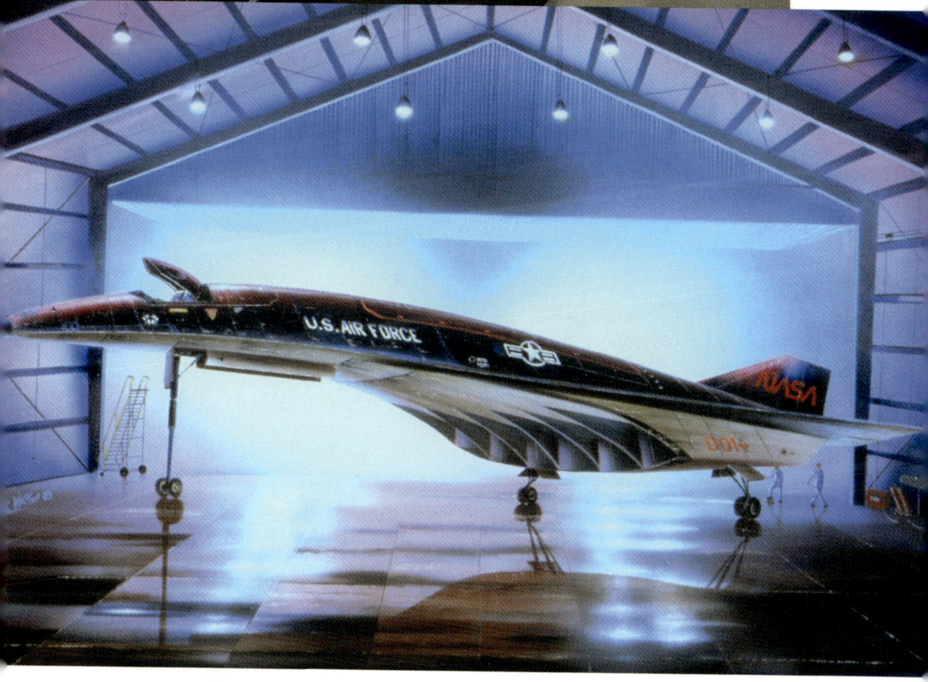
U.S. AIR FORCE
NASA

Travel Inventions Time Line

Would you like to know how travel has changed from the early

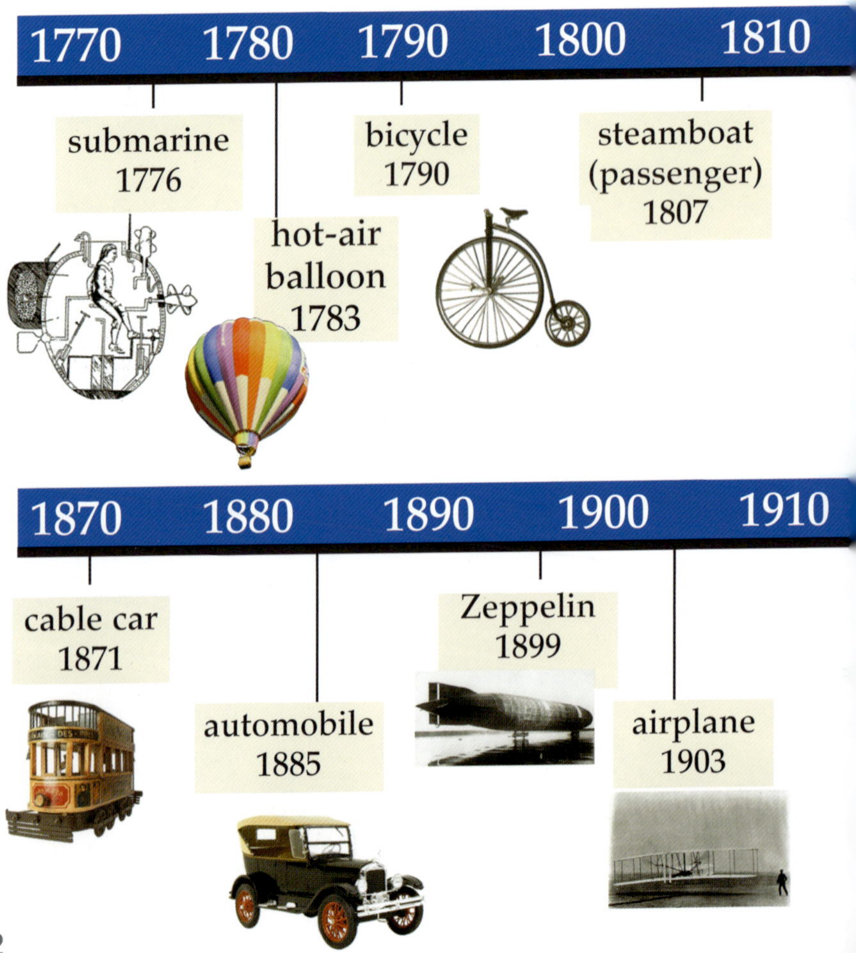

1770
1780
1790
1800
1810
submarine 1776
hot-air balloon 1783
bicycle 1790
steamboat (passenger) 1807
1870
1880
1890
1900
1910
cable car 1871
automobile 1885
Zeppelin 1899
airplane 1903

United States to now? Take a look at this time line. It will show you.

1820 1830 1840 1850 1860 1870

passenger train 1825

glider 1853

subway 1863

motorcycle 1867

1920 1930 1940 1950 1960 1970

jet plane 1939

helicopter 1940

spaceship (people landing on the moon) 1969

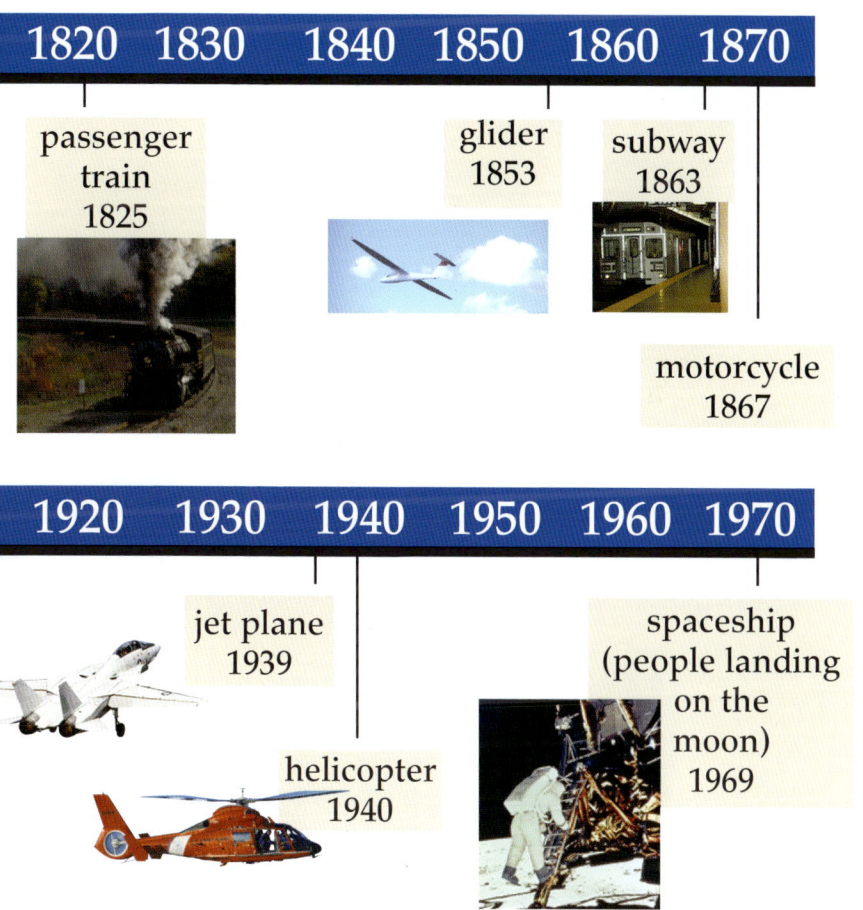

Glossary

 airplane
 automobile
 boat
 bus
 carriage
 glider
 helicopter
 hot-air balloon
 ship
 sleigh
 spaceship
 submarine
 subway
 train
 wagon